W9-BON-521

PRIMARY SOURCES OF
FAMOUS PEOPLE IN AMERICAN HISTORY™

JESSE JAMES

WESTERN BANK ROBBER
LEGENDARIO BANDIDO DEL OESTE AMERICANO

KATHLEEN COLLINS

TRADUCCIÓN AL ESPAÑOL:
TOMÁS GONZÁLEZ

rosen central
Primary Source™
Editorial Buenas Letras™
The Rosen Publishing Group, Inc., New York

Published in 2004 by The Rosen Publishing Group, Inc.
29 East 21st Street, New York, NY 10010

First Bilingual Edition 2004
First English Edition 2004

Cataloging Data

Collins, Kathleen.
Jesse James / Kathleen Collins; translation into Spanish Tomás González.— 1st ed.
    v. cm. — (Famous people in American history)
Contents: Jesse James's early life — Jesse James and the James Gang — Wanted, dead or alive — The end of a famous outlaw — Making of a legend.
ISBN 0-8239-4160-4 (library binding)
1. James, Jesse, 1847–1882—Juvenile literature. 2. Outlaws—West (U.S.)—Biography—Juvenile literature. 3. Frontier and pioneer life—West (U.S.)—Juvenile literature. 4. West (U.S.)—History—1860-1890—Juvenile literature. 5. West (U.S.)—Biography—Juvenile literature. [1. James, Jesse, 1847–1882. 2. Robbers and outlaws. 3. Frontier and pioneer life—West (U.S.) 4. West (U.S.)—History—1860-1890. 5. Spanish Language Materials—Bilingual]
I. Title. II. Series: Primary sources of famous people in American history. Bilingual.
F594.J27C65 2004
364.15'52'092—dc21

Manufactured in the United States of America

Photo credits: cover Hulton/Archive/Getty Images; p. 5 Library of Congress Prints and Photograph Division, HABS,MO,11-SAJOE,9-1; pp. 7, 23, 27 Library of Congress Prints and Photographs Division; pp. 9 (X-22154), 15 (X-21822) Denver Public Library, Western History Collection; p. 11 © Bettmann/Corbis; p. 13 Collection of David Carroll; p. 17 courtesy of Northfield Historical Society, Northfield, MN; p. 19 courtesy of Missouri State Archives; p. 21 courtesy of State Historical Society of Missouri, Columbia; p. 25 © Corbis; p. 29 Center for Popular Music, MTSU

Designer: Thomas Forget; Photo Researcher: Rebecca Anguin-Cohen

CONTENTS

CONTENIDO

JESSE JAMES'S EARLY LIFE

1

Jesse James was born in Missouri on September 5, 1847. His father, Robert, was a minister. Robert James was also a farmer. He died in 1851. In 1857, Jesse's mother, Zerelda, married a farmer and doctor named Reuben Samuels. Jesse and his older brother, Frank, were raised as farm boys.

PRIMEROS AÑOS DE JESSE JAMES

1

Jesse James nació en Misuri el 5 de septiembre de 1847. Su padre, Robert James, fue sacerdote y granjero. Robert murió en 1851. In 1857, Zerelda, madre de Jesse, se casó con Reuben Samuels, que era médico y granjero. Jesse y su hermano mayor, Frank, se criaron en una granja.

When Jesse James was growing up, he and his family lived in this house in St. Joseph, Missouri.

De joven, Jesse James vivió junto con su familia en esta casa en St. Joseph, Misuri.

When Jesse James was sixteen, the Civil War broke out. The Civil War, which started in 1861 and ended in 1865, was a very bloody battle. Sometimes friends would kill each other because they were on different sides. Jesse's parents were Confederates. Jesse and his brother were on the side of the South, too.

Cuando Jesse James tenía dieciséis años de edad estalló la Guerra Civil. Esta guerra, que empezó en 1861 y terminó en 1865, fue muy sangrienta. A veces los amigos se mataban porque pertenecían a bandos diferentes. Los padres de Jesse eran del bando del Sur, o confederados. Jesse y su hermano también estaban a favor de los confederados.

This 1862 photo shows Union soldiers at a signal station on Elk Mountain in Maryland during the Battle of Antietam.

Foto de 1862 donde aparecen soldados de La Unión en las montañas Elk de Maryland durante la batalla de Antietam.

7

During the Civil War, Jesse's family home was attacked by enemies from the North. This made Jesse angry. He decided to become an outlaw. In 1862, Jesse and Frank joined a band of Confederate rebels in Missouri and Kansas. They attacked farms and communities that were on the side of the North.

Durante la Guerra Civil, la casa de James fue atacada por el bando del Norte. Esto enojó mucho a Jesse, quien decidió convertirse en bandido. En 1862, Jesse y Frank se unieron a una banda de rebeldes confederados de Misuri y Kansas. Atacaban granjas y pueblos que apoyaban al ejército del Norte.

Jesse James and his brother, Frank, posed for this portrait sometime between 1866 and 1876.

Jesse James y su hermano Frank posaron para esta fotografía entre 1866 y 1876.

2 JESSE JAMES AND THE JAMES GANG

In 1866, Jesse and Frank formed their own band of outlaws. A Confederate rebel named Cole Younger and his brothers joined the James brothers. They were known as the James Gang. There were about twelve members. Jesse was the gang leader. They committed robberies and killed people in several states, including Iowa, Alabama, and Texas.

---

2 JESSE JAMES Y SU PANDILLA

En 1866, Jesse y Frank formaron su propia pandilla. Un rebelde confederado llamado Cole Younger y sus hermanos se unieron a los hermanos James. Se la llamó la "Pandilla de los James" y tenía alrededor de doce miembros. Jesse era su líder. Robaban y mataban gente en varios estados, entre ellos Iowa, Alabama y Texas.

Cole Younger was born in Jackson County, Missouri, in 1844.

Cole Younger nació en el condado de Jackson, Misuri, en 1844.

On February 13, 1866, Jesse and Frank robbed a bank in Liberty, Missouri. They stole thousands of dollars and killed a bystander. Many people say it was the first bank robbery to take place during the day. The James Gang became famous all around the United States. Some people wrote stories and songs about them.

El 13 de febrero de 1866, Jesse y Frank asaltaron un banco en Liberty, Misuri. Robaron miles de dólares y mataron a un transeúnte. Muchos dijeron que ése había sido el primer robo de banco de la historia realizado a la luz del día. La Pandilla de los James se hizo famosa en todo el país y se escribieron cuentos y canciones sobre ella.

These never-before-published cards feature gang members Jim Younger *(top)* and his brother, Cole Younger *(bottom)*.

En estas tarjetas nunca antes publicadas aparecen Jim Younger *(arriba)* y su hermano Cole *(abajo)*, miembros de la Pandilla de los James.

The James Gang continued to steal gold and money from stagecoaches, stores, banks, and people from Iowa to Alabama and Texas. On July 21, 1873, they robbed a train for the first time on the Rock Island Railroad in Adair, Iowa. They would continue their lives of crime for more than fifteen years.

La Pandilla de los James siguió robando oro y dinero de las diligencias, las tiendas, los bancos y la gente, desde Iowa hasta Alabama y Texas. El 21 de julio de 1873 asaltó por primera vez un tren, de la línea *Rock Island Railroad*, en Adair, Iowa. Los miembros de la pandilla dedicaron sus vidas al crimen durante más de quince años.

In the 1800s, horse-drawn stagecoaches were used to take people to places where trains couldn't go. Bandits, like Jesse James, held up stagecoaches and robbed the passengers.

En la década de 1800 se utilizaban diligencias para transportar a la gente a los lugares donde no llegaban los trenes. Bandidos, como Jesse James, asaltaban las diligencias y robaban a los pasajeros.

3 WANTED: DEAD OR ALIVE

On September 7, 1876, the James Gang robbed a bank in Northfield, Minnesota. Many people were killed during the robbery. Three members of the gang were captured and put in jail for life. Only Jesse and Frank James escaped. After the robbery, the brothers hid in Nashville, Tennessee, for more than three years.

---

3 SE BUSCA: VIVO O MUERTO

El 7 de septiembre de 1876, la Pandilla de los James robó un banco en Northfield, Minnesota. Muchas personas murieron durante el robo. Tres miembros de la pandilla fueron capturados y encarcelados de por vida. Sólo Jesse y Frank James escaparon. Después del robo, los hermanos se ocultaron en Nashville, Tennessee, durante más de tres años.

REWARD!

– DEAD OR ALIVE –

$5,000.00 x x will be paid for the capture of the men who robbed the bank at

NORTHFIELD, MINN.

They are believed to be Jesse James and his Band, or the Youngers.

All officers are warned to use precaution in making arrest. These are the most desperate men in America.

Take no chances! Shoot to kill!!

J. H. McDonald,
SHERIFF

After the famous robbery of the Northfield bank in 1876, this "wanted" poster was put up to help capture the dangerous outlaws.

Después del famoso robo del banco en *Northfield*, se colocó este cartel para ayudar a la captura de los bandidos.

In 1880, a lawyer named William H. Wallace wanted the outlaws to be arrested. Governor Thomas T. Crittenden of Missouri offered a $10,000 reward for the capture of the James brothers. He would pay the reward if the brothers were brought to him either dead or alive.

In 1880, el abogado William H. Wallace exigió el arresto de los bandidos. El gobernador Thomas T. Crittenden de Misuri ofreció $10.000 de recompensa por la captura de los hermanos James. Pagaría el dinero a quien le trajese a los hermanos, vivos o muertos.

Thursday July 28th 1881.

The Governor issued the following
Proclamation.

State of Missouri
Executive Department

Whereas, it has been made known to me, as the governor of the State of Missouri, that certain parties, whose names are to me unknown, have confederated and banded themselves together for the purpose of committing robberies and other depredations within this state; and

Whereas, said parties did on or about the eighth day of October 1879, stop a train near Glendale in the county of Jackson in said state and with force and violence take, steal and carry away the money and other express matter being carried thereon; and

Whereas, on the 15th day of July, 1881, said parties and their confederates did stop a train upon the line of the Chicago Rock Island and Pacific Railway Company, near Winston, in the county of Daviess in said state, and with force and violence take, steal and carry away the money and other express matter being carried thereon; and

Whereas, in perpetration of the robbery last aforesaid, the parties engaged therein did kill and murder one William Westfall the conductor of the train aforesaid, together with one John McCulloch who was at the time in the employ of said company then on said train; and

Whereas, Frank James and Jesse W. James stand indicted in the circuit court of Daviess county in the state aforesaid for the murder of John W. Sheets; and

Whereas, the parties engaged in the robberies and murders aforesaid, and each of them, have fled from justice and have absconded and secreted themselves:

Now Therefore, in consideration of the premises, and in lieu of all other rewards heretofore offered for the arrest or conviction of the parties aforesaid or either of them by any person or corporation I, Thomas T. Crittenden, governor of the state

In this letter, Governor Crittenden offers a $10,000 reward for the capture of the James brothers.

En esta carta, el gobernador Crittenden ofrece $10.000 de recompensa por la captura de los hermanos James.

4 THE END OF A FAMOUS OUTLAW

Jesse was living in St. Joseph, Missouri, with his wife and children. Jesse had married Zerelda Mimms on April 24, 1874. It may have seemed like he was living a quiet life with his family. But he was not finished with his outlaw life. He was pretending that his name was Thomas Howard so that he would not get caught.

———◆◆◆———

4 EL FINAL DE UN BANDIDO

Jesse estaba viviendo en St. Joseph, Misuri, con su mujer y sus hijos. Se había casado con Zerelda Mimms el 24 de abril de 1874. Daba la impresión de que se había dedicado a vivir una vida tranquila con su familia. Sin embargo, su carrera de bandido aún no había terminado. Para no ser atrapado utilizaba el nombre de Thomas Howard.

Zerelda Amanda Mimms is most famous for being the wife of Jesse James. Zee, as she was called, was born in Kentucky.

Zerelda Amanda Mimms es famosa por ser la esposa de Jesse James. Zee, como la llamaban, nació en Kentucky.

A man named Robert Ford was a member of Jesse's gang. He wanted to try to get the reward money all for himself. He also wanted to be known as the person who killed the famous Jesse James. He went to Jesse's home in St. Joseph, Missouri, in the spring of 1882.

———◆◆◆———

Uno de los miembros de la Pandilla de los James se llamaba Robert Ford. Quería ganarse él solo el dinero de la recompensa que ofrecían por Jesse. También quería ser conocido como la persona que mató al famoso Jesse James. En la primavera de 1882 fue a casa de Jesse, en St. Joseph, Misuri.

Robert Newton Ford said he was Jesse's friend, but he had other plans. Ford told Governor Crittenden that he would capture Jesse James.

Robert Newton Ford decía ser amigo de Jesse, pero tenía otros planes. Ford le dijo al gobernador Crittenden que capturaría a James.

Jesse invited Robert Ford and his brother Charley into his home to plan another robbery in Missouri. Jesse trusted Ford. He even took off his guns and put them on a table. While Jesse turned his back, Ford shot Jesse and killed him. Jesse James died on April 3, 1882.

Jesse invitó a su casa a Robert Ford y a su hermano, Charley, para planear otro robo en Misuri. Jesse confiaba en Ford. Incluso se quitó sus pistolas y las puso sobre una mesa. Cuando Jesse le dio la espalda, Ford le disparó y lo mató. Jesse James murió el 3 de agosto de 1882.

This 1882 photo shows the dead body of Jesse James. He was thirty-four years old.

Fotografía de 1882 del cadáver de Jesse James. Jesse murió a los treinta y cuatro años de edad.

5 MAKING OF A LEGEND

In the end, Robert Ford did not get the reward. Governor Crittenden had offered Ford a pardon if he killed Jesse. Ford was found guilty of murder, but the governor kept his promise and let him go free. Frank James gave himself up six months after his brother Jesse died.

5 EL NACIMIENTO DE UNA LEYENDA

Al final, Robert Ford no recibió la recompensa. El gobernador Crittenden le prometió el perdón si mataba a Jesse. A Ford lo hallaron culpable de asesinato, pero el gobernador cumplió su promesa e hizo que saliera libre. Frank James se entregó a la justicia seis meses después de la muerte de su hermano Jesse.

This grouping of photos, from 1882, shows some of the main elements in what became known as the legend of Jesse James.

Estas fotografías de 1882 muestran algunos de los elementos de lo que se conoce como la leyenda de Jesse James.

Many legends and songs were written about Jesse James and the James Gang. Some people thought of them as heroes because people said they stole from the rich and gave to the poor. But Jesse most likely made up that myth himself. Today, Jesse and Frank James are among the best-known Americans in history.

Muchas leyendas y canciones se han escrito sobre Jesse James y la Pandilla de los James. Algunos los consideraron héroes, porque según ellos robaban a los ricos para darles a los pobres. Pero lo más probable es que ése haya sido un mito creado por el propio Jesse. Hoy, Jesse y Frank James se encuentran entre los estadounidenses más conocidos de la historia.

Jesse James was so interesting that people kept on writing songs about him long after he was dead.

La vida de Jesse James fue tan interesante que la gente siguió escribiendo canciones sobre él mucho después de su muerte.

TIMELINE

1847—Jesse James is born in Missouri on September 5.

1866—Jesse and Frank form the James Gang. They rob a bank in Liberty, Missouri, on February 13.

1876—The James Gang robs a bank in Northfield, Minnesota.

1882—Robert Ford kills Jesse James on April 3.

1861-1865— The Civil War.

1873—The James Gang robs a train on the Rock Island Railroad.

1880—Governor Crittenden offers a reward for the capture of the James brothers.

CRONOLOGÍA

1847—Jesse James nace en Misuri el 5 de septiembre.

1866—Jesse y Frank forman la Pandilla de los James. El 13 de febrero roban un banco en Liberty, Misuri.

1876—La Pandilla de los James roba un banco en Northfield, Minnesota.

1882—El 3 de abril Robert Ford mata a Jesse James.

1861-1865—Se produce la Guerra Civil.

1873—La Pandilla de los James roba un tren de la línea *Rock Island Railroad*.

1880—El gobernador Crittenden ofrece una recompensa por la captura de los hermanos James.

GLOSSARY

capture (KAP-chur) To take a person by force.

Confederacy (kun-FEH-duh-reh-see) The eleven Southern states that declared themselves separate from the United States in 1860 and 1861.

loyal (LOY-uhl) Faithful to a person or an idea.

myth (MITH) A story that people make up to explain events.

outlaw (OWT-law) A criminal, especially one who is running away from the law.

pardon (PAR-duhn) To excuse someone who did something wrong.

rebel (REH-bul) A person who fought for the South during the Civil War.

reward (reh-WARD) Something you get in return for doing something good.

WEB SITES

Due to the changing nature of Internet links, the Rosen Publishing Group, Inc., has developed an online list of Web sites related to the subject of this book. This site is updated regularly. Please use this link to access the list:

http://www.rosenlinks.com/fpah/jjam

GLOSARIO

bandido (-a) Un delincuente, especialmente uno que escapa de la justicia.

capturar Apoderarse de alguien por la fuerza.

Confederación (la) Los once estados del Sur que se declararon independientes de Estados Unidos en 1860 y 1861.

leal Que es fiel a una persona o una idea.

mito (el) Historia que la gente inventa para explicar los acontecimientos.

perdonar Dejar de castigar a alguien que hizo algo malo.

rebelde (el, la) Persona que luchó por el Sur durante la Guerra Civil. Persona que no obedece a la autoridad establecida.

recompensa (la) Algo que obtienes por hacer una buena acción.

SITIOS WEB

Debido a las constantes modificaciones en los sitios de Internet, Rosen Publishing Group, Inc., ha desarrollado un listado de sitios Web relacionados con el tema de este libro. Este sitio se actualiza con regularidad. Por favor, usa este enlace para acceder a la lista:

http://www.rosenlinks.com/fpah/jjam

INDEX

ABOUT THE AUTHOR

Kathleen Collins was born in Rochester, New York. She is a writer and researcher who now lives in New York City. She loves to learn and write about American history.

ÍNDICE

ACERCA DEL AUTOR

Kathleen Collins nació en Rochester, Nueva York. Es escritora e investigadora, y actualmente vive en la ciudad de Nueva York. Es aficionada a estudiar la historia de Estados Unidos y escribir sobre ella.